My First Book

Pictures by Tadasu Izawa and Shigemi Hijikata

Publishers · GROSSET & DUNLAP · New York

Library of Congress Catalog Card Number: 82-84335
ISBN: 0-448-12287-1

Illustrations Copyright © 1971 by Tadasu Izawa and Copyright
© 1972, 1973 by Tadasu Izawa and Shigemi Hijikata
through the management of Dairisha, Inc. Printed and bound in Japan
by Zokeisha Publications, Ltd., Roppongi, Minato-ku, Tokyo.

Contents

The Alphabet

A a

Apple

B b

Ball

C c

Cat

D d

Dog

E e

Elephant

F f

Frog

G g
Giraffe

H h
House

7

I i

Indian

J j

Jelly

K k

Kite

L l

Leaves

9

M m

Mouse

N n

Nest

O o

Owl

P p

Pig

11

Q q
Queen

R r
Rabbit

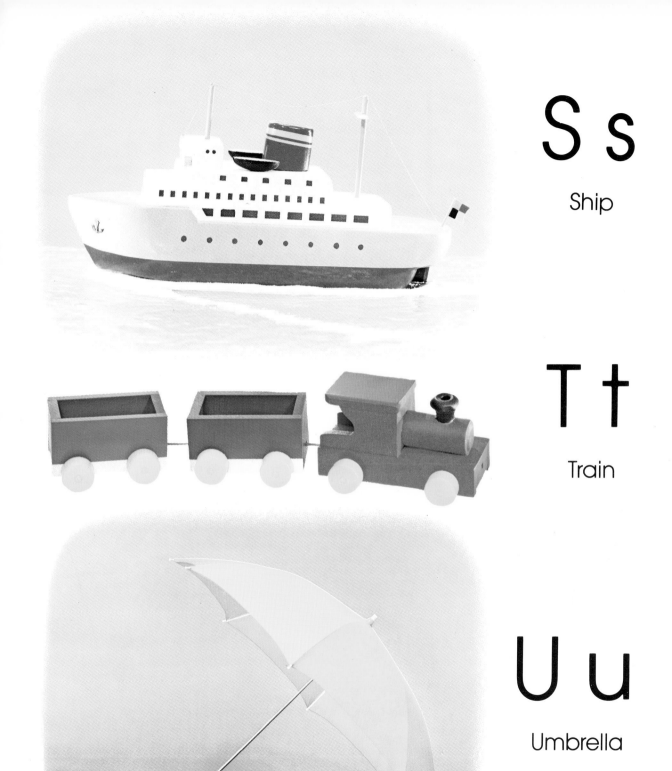

S s
Ship

T t
Train

U u
Umbrella

13

V v
Vase

W w
Wheel

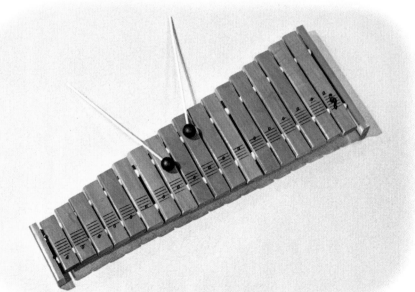

X x
Xylophone

Y y

Yarn

Z z

Zebra

15

First Words

What do you see in
the playroom?
Say the words.

girl

dollhouse

chair

pictures

toy chest

oll

book

kitten

ball

17

What do you see in
the kitchen?
Say the words.

boy

cookies

milk

chair

table

puppy

19

picture

bed

lamp

rug

20

clock

book

What do you see in
the bedroom?
Say the words.

rain

umbrella

woman

fence

house

What do you see on
the street?
Say the words.

man

What do you see on
the farm?
Say the words.

clouds

farmer

tractor

barn

cow

horse

25

birds

tree

grass

nest

sky

squirrel

flowers

What do you see in
the country?
Say the words.

Colors

The grass is
GREEN,
The sky is
BLUE,

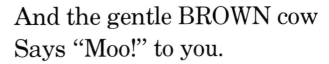

And the gentle BROWN cow
Says "Moo!" to you.

Easter eggs to color—
What fun it is to do!
We'll paint them pretty colors,
Like PURPLE, PINK, and BLUE.

A delicious ORANGE carrot
And GREEN lettuce to eat
Are the vegetables all bunnies
Think are a special treat.

Peppermint canes,
Striped RED and WHITE,
And BROWN sugar cookies
Are a Christmas delight.

On a shaggy
GREEN carpet,
Chasing a bright
RED ball,

A playful
ORANGE kitten
Has the most
fun of all.

A pair of
YELLOW paddles
And a gleaming
RED canoe

Will take these
friends across
the lake,
The lake that
looks so BLUE.

Numbers

1
One
Boy

2
Two
Puppies

3
Three
Kittens

4
Four
Butterflies

5
Five
Cups

6
Six
Chairs

7
Seven
Ducks

8
Eight
Balloons

9
Nine
Flowers

10
Ten
Crayons

Telling Time

Hickory, dickory, dock,
The mouse looks at the clock.
The sun is rising. My, it's red!
It's time to hop right out of bed.
What time is it?

Hickory, dickory, dock,
The mouse looks at the clock.

Time for breakfast! Time to eat
Cereals of oats, rice, corn, or wheat.
What time is it?

Hickory, dickory, dock,
The mouse looks at the clock.
Now it's time to play outside
And perhaps go for a ride.
What time is it?

Hickory, dickory, dock,
The mouse looks at the clock.
Now to the market Mother must go
To shop for things that make us grow.
    What time is it?

Hickory, dickory, dock,
The mouse looks at the clock.
Mother takes needle and thread—and sews
All of her many children's clothes.
    What time is it?

Hickory, dickory, dock,
The mouse looks at the clock.
Mother mixes eggs, milk, sugar, and flour
To bake a cake that will take an hour.
   What time is it?

Hickory, dickory, dock,
The mouse looks at the clock.
The hour is over, the cake is done.
Now eating it will be even more fun!
  What time is it?

Hickory, dickory, dock.
The mouse looks at the clock.
Daddy comes home from work to say
"What has everyone done today?"
  What time is it?

Hickory,
dickory,
dock,
The mouse looks
at the clock.
A story to read
is also fun,
And so another
day is done.
What time
is it?

Look at the clock
in your house.
It's BEDTIME,
isn't it?

Big and Little

The BIG cow
moves toward the
farmer's barn.
"Moo!" she says.
It will soon be
milking time.

A TINY green
frog sits atop a
wooden fence. The
frog is SMALL, but
he can jump far.

At the country fair, boys and girls cheer and clap their hands as a HUGE balloon is filled with hot air. Soon the balloonists are floating high above the crowd.

One girl holds on tightly to the string of her own LITTLE balloon. She doesn't want it to float away, too!

The BIG steam shovel scoops up LARGE heavy rocks and drops them into a dump truck making BIG rumbling sounds.

The LITTLE boy can use his LITTLE shovel to fill up his sand pail and can have just as much fun as the BIG man who runs the BIG steam shovel.

BIG, THICK ropes hold the BIG ship close to the dock. The ship cannot move away.

The LITTLE boy pulls the THIN string tied to his LITTLE toy boat—and makes it move anywhere he wants in the LITTLE pond.

A GIANT rocket carrying men and machines blasts off for the moon, thousands of miles away.

A SMALL skyrocket shoots up into the sky. It doesn't go very far and soon it bursts into a shower of lots of TINY sparkles.

The world is a
BIG place. It has
BIG mountains,
BIG oceans, BIG
buildings, and
many, many
people.

But it looks just like a LITTLE blue
marble moving through the darkness to
a man walking on the moon or riding in
a spaceship!

Do's and Don'ts

Always be kind to animals. If you have pets, feed them and take good care of them. A dog will wag its tail. A cat will purr. That's how they say, "Thank you."

No one likes to see a dirty face and
dirty hands. Wash with soap and
water!

When you must ask for something,
say "Please." And when you get it, say
"Thank you."

Share your
toys. It's more
fun when lots of
boys and girls
are having fun!

Be helpful around the house. Put away your toys when you are through playing with them.

A frown on
your face makes
other people sad.

But a smile on
your face makes
other people
happy.

Always hold
on to Mommy's
or Daddy's hand
when crossing
the street.

Don't throw candy wrappers on the street. Do throw them into the litter basket or can.

Go to bed when it's bedtime. Have pleasant dreams. Tomorrow will be another busy day!

Best Friends

I see a friend. He is a MAILMAN.
He brings letters from people all over
the world. Letters tell you how your
friends are doing. He brings magazines
and books and packages, too.

I see another friend. He is a
POLICEMAN. He makes sure that
people are kept safe.
TWEE-E-E-E-EET! He blows his
whistle and waves his hands. He
is telling people it is safe to cross
the street.

I see another friend. He is a FIREMAN. When there is a fire, people call him quickly. He climbs upon a fire engine and hurries to the place where the fire is. He shoots water from a hose onto the flames until there is no more fire.

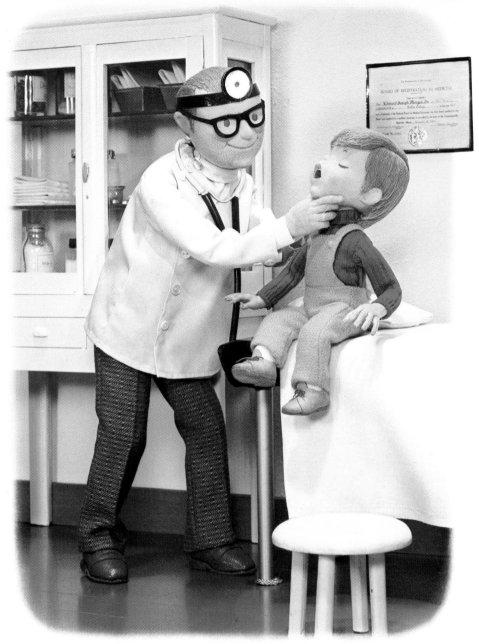

I see another friend. He is a
DOCTOR. When people are sick, or
hurt, they come to him. He examines
them carefully to find out what is
wrong. He gives people medicine to
make them well again.

I see another friend. She is a
NURSE. She helps the doctor—and
she helps people get well, too. She
takes care of getting things or doing
things that they need.

I see another friend. He is a BUS DRIVER.
Some bus drivers drive children to school. Other
bus drivers drive people to work—or to other
places they may want to go. A bus holds many
people, so a bus driver must drive carefully.

I see the BOYS and GIRLS I play with. We play games together and have fun. Sometimes we go on a picnic. Sometimes we play on the seesaw or go down slides. Sometimes we go on rides, like a merry-go-round.

I see another friend. She is a
TEACHER. She has a class of many
boys and girls in a school. The teacher
shows the boys and girls how to do
things with paper and pencils and
crayons. It's so much fun!

MOMMY and DADDY are my special friends, because they love me very much.

All of my friends are friends of Mommy's and Daddy's, too. And isn't it nice that we can all be friends...with everybody!